BURNING BARREL

Poems

by

Natalli M. Amato

Finishing Line Press
Georgetown, Kentucky

BURNING BARREL

Poems

ACKNOWLEDGMENTS

Publisher: Leah Huete de Maines
Editor: Christen Kincaid
Cover Art: *Study of Mushrooms* (1880) by Mary Vaux Walcott, CC0 1.0
Author Photo: Alex Davidson
Cover Design: Elizabeth Maines McCleavy

Order online: www.finishinglinepress.com
also available on amazon.com

Author inquiries and mail orders:
Finishing Line Press
P. O. Box 1626
Georgetown, Kentucky 40324
U. S. A.

Table of Contents

For Lena, for taking the long way around.

I would like to promise her that she will grow up with a sense of her cousins and of rivers and her great-grandmother's teacups, would like to pledge her a picnic on a river with fried chicken and her hair uncombed, would like to give her home for her birthday, but we live differently now.

—Joan Didion

Burning Barrel

We burned our garbage in autumn,
and other seasons, but this is what I remember best:

the rusty barrel,
its sharp metal so ready to flake away
like amber leaves from an oak.

Mother, black smoke coughed into your sky
while I breathed deep as if I were standing before your holy river.

Forgive me
if I still miss the smell.

Winter Dawn

Trees down to nothing but bark.
Pink sky seeped through the branches.
Oh, how I loved you, sharp air,
ice atop the snow,
mittens not quite warm enough,
as I walked down the drive
to retrieve yesterday's mail.

For Joanne

Around the first autumn fire Joanne tells the story
of how she held me in her arms back when I had the bad colic
and Mom hadn't slept since before the ice storm.
They let the hot water tank run all the way out
filling the bathroom with steam
forcing December air into being kinder towards me.
A woman needs a friend the way that cabin needed a generator.
Who else looks into a subzero night
with the resolve to change its very composition?
Twenty years on and we feel it still—
the moment when the dry air first gives.

Storm Ripples

When I think of the lake
I remember it a widespread stillness
though it was not always so. There were afternoons
when I sat in Grandmother's picture window
with the screens open just enough for us to smell seaweed
inside the cottage. And then there was Aunt Wendy
who swore she could spot a storm
by the texture of the lake's surface; how it changed
from ripples stretching thin and long to the curt,
cropped kind. Storm Ripples!
She'd shout for the kids.
Through binoculars we squinted for those lines
as if they were rainbows
we had to crane our necks to see.

Air Asphyxiation

This is the oldest slaughter method for fish and is considered inhumane because it can take the fish over an hour to die.
—Fish Slaughter, Wikipedia

We dug holes twice our size
and called that fun; then cried
when the sand absorbed the water we poured and
the minnows we dug these homes for
twitched in synchronized exasperation
on the sandy bottom.

For Jaid

We sat criss-cross applesauce as we called it then
on your grandmother's carpet floor while the Singer hummed
and she explained how to thread the needle
and do something with a bobbin.

Your grandmother handed us squares
to pin on the fabric board.
We thumbed those 4x4 monuments to right angles
not knowing how to arrange them;
not knowing there's an art in deciding
one thing's place among the others.

Nightsong

The window screen need not be closed tonight.
Onshore wind pours through porous curtains.
A cotton sheet wraps coolness around skin
still synthesizing July sun.

I breathe air made for cicada chants
while beneath the window lunar water pushes
stone against stone
then folds into itself.

When sleep comes, water sounds remain.
Crests breaking, scooping stones in the trough.

Archer

When the neighbor boy
brings you out to the woods to drink
from the plastic vodka bottle he hides
beneath a heap of last year's autumn leaves,
he has forgotten the rabbit
that ran in front of the target
he had aimed for with his bow,
his arrow—how the rabbit hopped
hopped around the backyard, arrow
in its side. He has forgotten
how he cried then. He has forgotten
you saw.

Waiting

Humid air hangs close to skin;
it lands with the horsefly
on the nape of my neck.
I sit on the needs-staining porch
counting owlet moths
hovering around the citronella candle.
Damp bathing suits dangle from the railing
drip-dripping what is left of the day
onto dark grass.
In the driveway, the neighbor kids
get into a box of pop snaps.
They pelt them now
against our shared plot of pavement.
Small splat,
       small splat,
              small splat.
Their mother's fork and spoon wind chime
chimes on offshore wind.
I do remember the storms
that left her silver strewn across the lawn
but I admit I did not bring my body
to the water
when it was right there
falling.

Autumn Moon

November brings Orion—
I no longer see Cygnus
in the branches of the backyard oak.

This is a different yard,
remember.

The Sea of Tranquility
is clear to the eye.

I recall times before the knowing
of proper names—

When mother took
me by a mitten hand
and said, look there—
old man in the moon.

Watching Grandfather on the John Deere

Grandfather mows the lawn for the third time since Tuesday.
There is something to be said for the human comfort of repetition, yes,

but more so for the pleas we make even when we know
they cannot be answered.

I'm not sure who he does his bargaining with

      Time, God, John Deere, Grass,

or if the differentiation matters

but that is what each lap up and down up and down is.

One more afternoon among the smell of cut grass.
One more afternoon.

Lake Talk

Across the bay a mother puts hot dogs on the grill.
She asks her backyard who wants one.
The old men down the shoreline
go on spitting
      Goddamn geese
           Goddamn geese
while in the water out past the boat hoists
the teenage girls talk in their cadence of trust:
Voices catching at the good parts,
trying out words too big for the dinner table,
fitting an arms-raised hallelujah in between the syllables of the other's name
      Julia!
           Julia!
I look up from my book.
Let me bear witness to praise.

We Go See Willie Nelson

I tell you we had to slug those beers
after the September sun went down
it left the amphitheater to purple coolness
never quite reaching nighttime black
thank the stage lights
beer stands
cell phones too
cell phones where lighters used to be
so we had to slug those beers
let them slosh inside our bellies as we dance
when Willie brings his body across the stage
I need to see three of him
God honest
there's got to be more than this one body
this one hollowed out body
save for the whistle it gives
when wind passes through

Broken Window

The old window screen let in bonfire smoke,
horseflies, calls from the neighbor kids.

Get a good wind going and it would pop
out of the sill's softened wood
onto the carpet with the rain.

When we spotted a ladybug
crawling the countertop,
we tried to count her spots
before our luck flew away.

Ontario Morning

Even the gulls are at rest
with wings tucked to their sides
standing on the elder rock
facing blue water in communion with blue sky
while the wind pushes small ripples across the lake's surface.

This is my hour to sit with pen and paper
though nothing comes besides Ontario breeze,
besides thank you.

Mother's Slivers

Mother's plastic serving bowl
could hold potato salad for thirteen
or both my soaking feet
depending on the afternoon.

No stinger, no sliver,
was too deep for her to pluck
from my peroxide puckered skin.

There she knelt,
tweezers pinched
between thumb and forefinger,
because I had walked without
the shoes she gave me.

Mother, you brought me here—
to the green grass,
to the clover,
to a full, needs-sanding porch.
Oh, how I had to
feel it:

The yellow of a dandelion
smushed beneath my toes—

the puncture.

When you dumped my dirtied water down the drain
and sent me back into the world with Neosporin's gloss,
you knew this.

And once the bowl was clean, returned,
you never took it down for yourself.

Tell me, now, what did you leave lodged
beneath your skin
when you picked your feet up

again and again
to follow me?

What alchemy is yours
that turned slivers into the sturdy trunk of a pine?

II.

In Brooklyn Heights

I took my longing out
for a drink on Henry Street.
I ordered a gin and tonic at a wine bar,
sucked it down through that obstacle of a straw
until it was just glass and ice.
When the girl behind the bar looked away
I reached inside the glass with my fingers,
shoveled cubes into my mouth.
I had brought a notebook with me
but never wrote a thing down.
Just chewed, chewed, chewed.

Navigation

Moths confuse porch lights for the starlight
that guided their ancestors' migrations.

In the morning I sweep their bodies into a dustpan.

If I ever think myself wise enough
to call these winged ones fools,
I must stop and call out, *sisters!*

There were years I mistook others for you.

Peeling

I bring the carrot peeler to the waxy skin
of butternut squash.
It comes off in chunks instead of ribbons
even after I adjust the wobbling blade.

Diana Ross' "On the Radio" plays on the turntable.
I hear my mother sing. She is not in this house.

I sing over her.
I sing over Diana.
I force a ribbon
where there isn't.
My finger bleeds.

In the Winter Night

I wake from the old dream—lost on the river.
Outside, snowflakes look like moths around the lamppost light.
I watch until I remember something close to summer's air.

Walking Down 5th Avenue I See a Ram 1500

No dings. No dung
clung to tires' indents.
Not so much as a gravel chunk
tucked between the bed's ridges.
I could key the damn thing
just to make it look like the half-ton beast
that carried me and the neighbor girls
when our ponytails were matted with lake water.

Again

Let me hear it

The crack of thunder
        a shotgun for the footrace
                between our fishing boat
                        and summer's first storm

The lone long holler you let out
        when we hit the first true back road
                rising up into the empty night
                        towards impossible stars

The snare of fireworks knocked onto sand
        never reaching higher than the reeds
                wailing railing almost detonating
                        our own gunpowder bodies

In the Sandflats, For Elena

You come from women who bring lasagna—
who walk into grief's house without knocking,
bold enough to pick up the place a little bit,
even do a few dishes, yelling,
Eat! Eat this now before it gets cold.
I did not know this is not how everyone does it.
I sat at my desk at my first job that wasn't waiting tables
while my boss talked of his friend's mother's death;
how he wanted to do something, maybe
I could order flowers.
So I found the Italian spot
that wasn't candlelight-dinners-for-two
but family-style: low prices in oversized font,
the kind of place where the website's red text clashes
against a green background. I had an antipasto and two sheet lasagnas delivered
and when I closed the browser window I saw your grandmother's kitchen stove:
Meat sauce going, hot oil jumping when cutlets touch the pan,
crucifix hanging overhead—
and I paused to thank Saint Anthony
for never letting us go without our hunger
even when the lost things were still missing.

Meditation

One yoga class in and I imagine myself a guru.
I can't even do one of those half handstands on the wall
or hold my *om* for a whole exhale.
When the class ends the instructor reads us a poem
on letting go of the self.
She leaves the room to pour tea.
The other yogis put their blocks away.
I sit here with all of my selves in one last embrace.
The twenty-year-old wants to stay and whine
about boys she thinks she loves and cities she thinks she hates
and she'd really love it if I could take her across the street to the bar
and order her a vodka ginger. Oh, she was insufferable to be,
always trying to yell over the party music,
always trying to proclaim something grand on paper
even when it wasn't true to how she felt.
The child is squished between us both.
She wants to leave us to go catch frogs
but I ask her, please,
stay and remember the butterfly.
Tell me again about the blue one
you saw that one October day with your mother—
the blue one you drew and drew and drew and never saw again.

Thoughts I Have While Volunteering at the Arts Center

We don't know
how to frame ourselves

Just look at the acrylic
of the Monarch Butterflies

A few centimeters of garden
on an 8x11

Overpowered
by a five-inch thick gold frame

For Lena

Friend, I almost called you mother
though Mother never spoke with wine
tripped words about how to sit with one's own blues
and say thank you to the hue.

Learning to walk past the dark barroom
of one's own creation was never the point.

Friend, you pulled up a chair and told the man to put on Joni.
Said you've got to learn to play that riff,
that warped indigo that comes
right before the one note sweet enough
to make you think fondly
even of the times
love passed by you.

I Wake for a Drink of Water

Shall I let it slip from my lips
until the water dribbles down my breast
the way the moon slid down my bare shoulders
those years ago with the old friends?

Ontario was always giving.

The floor is slick with four a.m.

I wonder what they have since learned
to do with the water.

Cousin, or For Joel When I Wouldn't Swim

Cousin,
there are children who grow up
without ever having played in the swamp.
And I don't mean Grampy's swamp—
        I'm talking any.

I mean they've never had a frog pee through their cupped hands
and their moms have never burned leaches from their skin with Bic lighters.

Cousin, I went twenty years before I learned the world could do this to a babe:
Plop them down on this Earth without a guarantee that a dragonfly will land
on their forearm.

There was a summer when I could feel it all ending before I had reason to.
I sat on Grandma's couch with my nose in a book and an ear in the aunties'
conversation about neighbors and husbands and bad hairdressers
and I told you no.
No, I won't help you blow up the plastic boat.
No, I won't carry the nets,
not the oars, either.
Three beaches over a toddler got green algae up his nose and died.
Want that to be you?

Cousin, I hope algae fills my lungs until it knows I am part of the wild.
I hope your scabs pucker with lakewater puss and tadpoles nibble the skin
from your feet.
I hope one day we are the swamp muck that sticks to a child's water shoes
tracking through the house her mother just cleaned
and the only thing left for us to do will be to rejoice
at being the residue of such glorious life.

III.

Picking Up Takeout

I go back to the old bar for a hamburger
only the boy on the grill is probably a stranger

I'd rather not know for sure
so I don't stick my head between the swing doors
the way I did when I had things to yell
and people to listen

The girl behind the bar never rolled silverware with me
she doesn't know who waited for me at shift's end
I don't know who she texts to get through hers

She knows I order extra BBQ and use an Amex

If this is a world where grace can dwell
Pearl would bust through the side door
shove a mop and a pail into my hands and
I would get out on that peel-paint deck
down on my knees scrubbing
scrubbing every last splatter of seagull shit
until pink shoulder skin flaked and fell
between the cracks of the wood planks
along with the dripping suds
along with the peeling paint

I Remember a Lecture on Signifiers and the Signified

When the swans crossed the river this morning
I resisted the urge to name each one
though ideas surely came.
You, with the tallest neck, reaching,
reaching, you must be the child I can sometimes still inhabit.
And you with outstretched wings, stationary body,
can be the novel I haven't written.
The slowest of the bevy—
was that you, the spring
when good people were lost?
I thought about this until my coffee was gone,
until their heads plunged underwater for their fill.
The only truthful thing to say was that these were swans
and they took away my breath.

Price Chopper, Alex Bay

Putting through the no-wake zone
I see a mom teach her boys how to hook a worm.

Connor is reading Tony Hoagland to me.
I hear the echo of every beautiful thing that I have heard to date.

It's a sound that makes me believe one day
I might want to be that woman on the dock.

Even though I don't believe in fishing.
Even though I have worn turtlenecks to wine bars in Brooklyn
where I adjusted my glasses and thought myself clever and made proclamations
like,

"Having children is a manifestation of all of our most selfish impulses."

We tie our ropes to the cleats.
Closer, now, it's clear these boys come from different men who

Am I raising two girls? Touch the damn fish, Patrick

she hates.

Morning With Blue Heron
for F.S.

When I edit my manuscript
I put the poems with that old plum pit hate
into the waste bin
with the to-do lists
bank statements
press releases.

Nothing
is more cringe-worthy
than the *self*.
I can say it now.
When the editor rejected my poem
about how immature I thought you were
I was appalled.

These were the days when I could not separate
who I was
from what I felt.
I mistook every thought born from emotion for art.

Looking back I should have written that you were kind
and I am grateful
you made it easy for me to let go.

This morning I saw a blue heron
lunge its beak into the lily pads
for a fish it did not catch.
He repeated this many times until the breeze picked up
and it was time to move
downriver.
In his absence
the surface of the river
remained in motion and
my lungs were cousin
to the rhythm.

Fireside With Childhood Friends

We pour honey in our gin while Prince tells us how the doves cried.
The music died and it will again.
Lightning bugs are visible from the willow tree's tallest branches.
We agree their lights were eye level when we were children.
The Milky Way spills across the backyard
like every jar of loose change that was ever kept is now turned over.
If only I could sift my fingers through those clusters.
I would look for the couch cushion quarter I had kept in my pocket
before it fell when we went running through the Rye.

The September Geese

The coffee is two or three sips from cold.
The gas fireplace is on, the blower is broken,
but still there is heat and the color orange in this room.
Outside the window the geese lift toward the sky.
It's late enough in the season that it's reasonable to think
we may not see our winged friends until the year next.
If they were our brothers, we'd send them off
with wishes and perhaps some snacks
and they may care whether we were there below.
This is not the way things are
so it is okay that we are satisfied
with a window-glimpse,
that we stay seated on the loveseat
talking about what we'll have for dinner tonight
while "Let It Be" plays on the turntable.

Autumn Walk

We walk by the lakeshore
passing September tree
by October tree.
It is now that yearly time
when it's believable,
the tragedy three years back,
when the local kids fell from the cliffside
and contrary to what was thought then,
it would have been better
had they never turned up on the shore
with the weeds, the lures, the beer cans.
What does it mean
that I keep my footing?
How easy
it could be
        roots bulging aboveground
lost.

Water Cycle

There is a world; you are of it.

Like the snow last night
so slow in its descent
it appeared to be floating.
You went on breathing
lungs filling, deflating,
in bone-silent harmony
with the crystalline flakes
turned liquid on your skin.

Sunoco Gas, Alex Bay

I'm twenty-three but I forgot my ID so I wait out in the parking lot
while Connor checks out with the beer like I'm sixteen again.
Was I ever sixteen?

No. I wired money to China
just to time travel in the eyes of the cashier at Mercer's gas station.

Across the street there's a sign for the hotel in which my sisters were conceived
years before my father was my father,
back when he was just the bartender.
If he left it was called a cigarette break.

The sky was somewhere close to me
before I started looking.

One Day Home Will Not Be My Home

The sun has risen and still
Ontario is grey. We have passed
The season of fishing boats and long-cast lines.
Bare trees. Empty cottages.
When will lake reclaim land? Not yet.
Not yet. This is autumn;
all things recede
except for the beach
which extends
like a bone protruding
from skin.

Reminder

Just outside, there are geese
lowering themselves from sky to lake
unbothered by frigid water
undisturbed by ice
making its way to the shore
on the helm of a wave
traveling from the open water.

Come March

There comes an evening when the windows do not fog.
You fold the wool blanket in half, in half once more,
so it fits in the closet where Christmas pillows are packed.
When you lay to take your rest, there is the sound from down below
of ice chunks clunking into rocks, into each other,
riding the water's vibrations, old bones popping.
In the morning you cast your fishing line gaze.
There is only water, water returned to itself.

Of the Earth

Towards the river I go
stepping on yesterday's leaves
that lie above the eternal soil.
Soil does not cry the way that I do
over this need to be an individual,
this longing to last.
Soil accepts its place in something larger—
matter breaking down in continuum
so that newness may never be perceived
even though it is renewed again, and again,
by death's unyielding changes.

Acknowledgments

I would like to thank the editors of the following publications where some of the poems in this collection first appeared, either in exact or a previous form.

BEATIFIC Magazine: "I Remember a Lecture on Signifiers and the Signified," "Lake Talk," "Winter Dawn"

Blueline: "The September Geese"

Brought to Sight & Swept Away: A Poetry Anthology About Time: "Watching Grandfather on the John Deere"

Chronogram: "Archer"

Darling Magazine: "Mother's Slivers," "Nightsong"

Funicular Magazine: "Price Chopper, Alex Bay"

Great Lakes Review: "Morning With Blue Heron"

Last Leaves Magazine: "Peeling," "Sunoco Gas, Alex Bay," "In Brooklyn Heights"
Lily Review: "Burning Barrel"

Peaceful Dumpling: "Reminder," "Thoughts While Volunteering at the Arts Center"

Speckled Trout Review: "Cousin, or For Joel When I Wouldn't Swim," "Picking up Takeout"

Without a Doubt: Poems Illustrating Faith: "Ontario Morning"

Words & Whispers Literary Magazine: "Of the Earth"

86 Logic: "For Lena"

Natalli Amato is a poet, fiction writer, and journalist from upstate New York. She is the author of the poetry collection *On a Windless Night*, which was published by Ra Press in 2019. She was awarded the Edwin T. Whiffen Poetry Prize as an undergraduate at Syracuse University, where she earned her degree in Sociology and Public Relations. Her poetry is deeply inspired by the North Country region of New York State where she grew up and continues to be drawn to. Her poetry has appeared in several anthologies and numerous literary publications, and she is a poetry reader for *Carve Magazine*. Natalli also writes for *Rolling Stone, Vice*, and *Taste of Country*. She is currently working on her first novel.

www.ingramcontent.com/pod-product-compliance
Lightning Source LLC
Chambersburg PA
CBHW021205090426
42740CB00008B/1233